AMAZING ART FORMS

# The Art of Painting

BY MARLEY RICHMOND

Kids Core

An Imprint of Abdo Publishing
abdobooks.com

**abdobooks.com**

Published by Abdo Publishing, a division of ABDO, PO Box 398166, Minneapolis, Minnesota 55439. Copyright © 2025 by Abdo Consulting Group, Inc. International copyrights reserved in all countries. No part of this book may be reproduced in any form without written permission from the publisher. Kids Core™ is a trademark and logo of Abdo Publishing.

Printed in the United States of America, North Mankato, Minnesota.
102024
012025

Cover Photo: Shutterstock Images
Interior Photos: Shutterstock Images, 4–5, 8, 13, 16 (paint blobs), 24, 29 (top); Ground Picture/Shutterstock Images, 6; Paul Signac/Niday Picture Library/Alamy, 10–11; Gianna Stadelmyer/Shutterstock Images, 15; Anastasiia Novikova/Shutterstock Images, 16 (color wheel); Alex Segre/Shutterstock Images, 18–19; Geoffrey Clements/Corbis Historical/VCG/Getty Images, 21; Bettmann/Getty Images, 23; Andrew Chin/Getty Images Entertainment/Getty Images, 26; Margouillat Photo/Shutterstock Images, 28 (top); Africa Studio/Shutterstock Images, 28 (bottom); Kuznetcov Konstantin/Shutterstock Images, 29 (bottom)

Editor: Haley Williams
Series Designer: Katharine Hale

**Library of Congress Control Number: 2024938360**

**Publisher's Cataloging-in-Publication Data**

Names: Richmond, Marley, author.
Title: The art of painting / by Marley Richmond
Description: Minneapolis, Minnesota: ABDO Publishing, 2025 | Series: Amazing art forms | Includes online resources and index.
Identifiers: ISBN 9781098295783 (lib. bdg.) | ISBN 9798384916789 (ebook)
Subjects: LCSH: Art--Juvenile literature. | Painting--Juvenile literature. | Art--Equipment and supplies--Juvenile literature. | Brushwork--Juvenile literature. | Painters in art--Juvenile literature. | Art--Technique--Juvenile literature. | Arts and history--Juvenile literature.
Classification: DDC 750--dc23

# CONTENTS

An easel is a stand that holds paper or a canvas upright while an artist is painting.

# Painting a Picture

Austin looked at the blank **canvas** in front of him. He could paint anything! Austin looked around and saw a vase with a sunflower in it. That was what he would paint.

Austin wanted to start with the brown center of the flower.

Some palettes have a hole so artists can hold them while painting.

He did not have any brown paint. But he knew how to mix colors. Austin squeezed yellow, red, and blue paint onto a **palette**. He mixed the three colors together to make brown.

Next, Austin painted the yellow petals of the flower. He noticed shadows between each petal. So he mixed a little brown paint with some yellow. This made the yellow paint darker. He used a paintbrush to blend the darker yellow into the petals where he saw shadows.

Austin kept working on his painting. He added more details. Eventually he was happy with it. He would let his painting dry and then hang it up.

## What Is Art?

People have been making art for tens of thousands of years. Early artworks included pictures that were painted on cave walls.

### Digital Art

Digital artists use technology to create artwork. Many digital art tools act like physical ones. For example, artists can blend colors in a digital art program as if they were blending paint on a palette. Technology gives artists the ability to try new techniques.

Thousands of years ago, early humans painted on cave walls.

Today, museums are full of art. Art is a way for people to express emotions, be creative, and make something beautiful.

Painting is one of the most popular art forms today. Artists use different types of paints, surfaces, and styles to create paintings. Some paintings are **abstract**. Others are realistic. Many are somewhere in between.

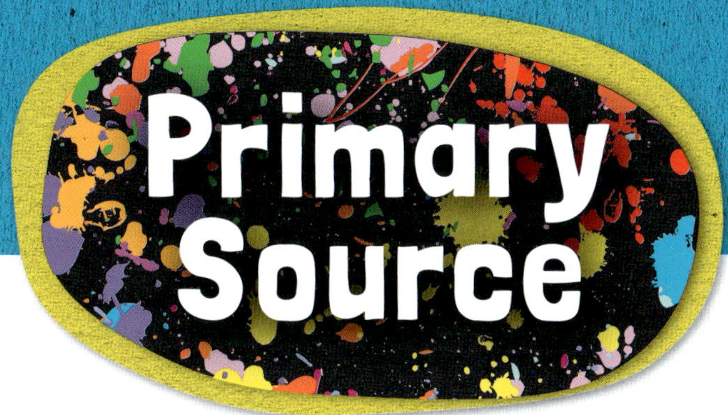


Georgia O'Keeffe was a famous painter. She talked about how painting helped her express her thoughts and feelings. O'Keeffe said:

> I found that I could say things with color and shapes that I couldn't say any other way—things that I had no words for.

Source: Chelsea Werner-Jatzke. "Inside Georgia O'Keefe: Abstract Variations." *Seattle Art Museum Blog*, 25 Mar. 2020, samblog.seattleartmuseum.org. Accessed 7 Feb. 2024.

## Point of View

What is the author's point of view on this topic? What is your point of view? Write a short essay about how they are similar and different.

Artists may experiment with different painting techniques. One technique some artists use is called pointillism.

# Paint Types and Techniques

Painters can choose from many mediums when making art. A medium is a material used to create art, such as a type of paint. Each medium creates a different effect. Some painters combine mediums. Others stick to one or two.

## Types of Paint

Acrylic paints are bright and **opaque**. These paints are water based. Painters can add more water to make the paint thinner and easier to spread. Acrylic paint dries quickly. Painters need to work fast. Once acrylic paint dries, it is difficult to remove. Artists often use acrylic paint on canvases.

Oil paints dry very slowly. That makes them easier to mix and blend. But they also require some special supplies. Painters use chemicals instead of water to thin their oil paints. They also use chemicals to wash their paintbrushes.

Watercolors are very different from acrylic and oil paints. These paints usually start dry. Painters add water to use them. Adding a lot of

Watercolor paint often comes in a palette that includes a variety of colors.

water makes the colors very light. Adding only a little water keeps the paint bright. Artists often use special watercolor paper for this medium. Watercolor paper does not **warp** when it gets wet.

Gouache (pronounced goo-AHSH) paint is thicker than watercolor. It is also more opaque. But gouache is easier to blend than acrylic paint. Gouache often starts wet. But if it dries out, painters can add water to make it mixable again. Painters should use thin layers of gouache. Thick layers of this paint often crack.

## Spray Painting

Spray paint covers large areas in thin, even coats of paint. Some artists use spray paint to make outdoor murals. Murals are works of art created on walls. Artists may use different types of spray cans to make clear lines or wide sprays of paint. They can also use stencils to create detailed shapes.

Painters may use different paintbrush sizes and shapes depending on what they are painting.

## Painting Techniques

One important skill for painters is learning to mix colors. Mixing colors allows artists to make different shades from just a few colors. Painters can also practice layering paint. By adding thin layers to a painting, artists create **dimension** in their work.

# Mixing Colors

Painters may practice mixing colors by creating a color wheel. Color wheels show what it looks like to mix two or more colors of paint together.

Painters also use specific techniques for different mediums. With watercolors, artists may choose to wet their paper before beginning to paint. Adding watercolors to a wet surface makes the paint **bleed**. This creates a blurry look.

Some painters may also use a mostly dry brush on a dry surface. This technique uses very little paint. It creates scratchy brushstrokes. Artists use dry brushing to paint trees or textured surfaces.

## Further Evidence

Look at the website below. Does it give any new evidence to support Chapter Two?

### Painting

abdocorelibrary.com/art-of-painting

Before cameras, artists painted portraits to show people's characteristics, personalities, and lives.

CHAPTER 3

# Artists and Museums

Over time, artists have created new styles of painting. Historians organize art history into different periods. Every period is known for its own style. There are famous painters from each period.

# Famous Painters

Leonardo da Vinci was an Italian painter. He lived during the late 1400s and early 1500s. His work was part of the Renaissance period. Many Renaissance paintings are realistic. Leonardo's most famous painting is the *Mona Lisa*.

In the 1800s, some painters created a style called Impressionism. This style focused on capturing the feeling of a scene rather than making it realistic. Claude Monet was a French Impressionist. He was known for painting landscapes. Monet's paintings are often colorful. His brushstrokes are easy to see.

Pablo Picasso was a Spanish painter. He lived from 1881 to 1973. Many of his famous works are Cubist. In this style, subjects are broken up

Some of Claude Monet's best-known paintings feature the water-lily pond at his home in Giverny, France.

and rearranged in abstract ways. One Cubist painting by Picasso is *The Weeping Woman.*

Modern artists are known for experimenting with their work. Frida Kahlo was a Mexican painter who lived during the early to mid-1900s.

Kahlo created many self-portraits. Her work celebrates women and Mexican culture.

Andy Warhol was another Modern artist. He lived during the early to late 1900s. Warhol created bold paintings of everyday objects. His style was known as Pop art.

Contemporary art is made by artists living today. One famous Contemporary painter is Kehinde Wiley. Wiley paints portraits of Black people using classic styles. Wiley's art makes his subjects look powerful. Yayoi Kusama is a Japanese painter. She is famous for using bright, colorful polka dots in her work. Kusama's artwork explores how **mental illness** can be expressed in art.

In 1925, Frida Kahlo began teaching herself how to paint while recovering from a serious injury.

The Metropolitan Museum of Art is also known as the Met. It is one of the largest art museums in the world.

## Popular Museums

There are many museums in the United States where people can see paintings. The Metropolitan Museum of Art is in New York City.

So is the Museum of Modern Art. The Art Institute of Chicago is in Illinois. These museums display paintings and other artwork from around the world.

There are also many famous museums outside of the United States. The Louvre is in Paris, France. This museum is so large that a person would need to spend 100 days there to see every piece of art. The *Mona Lisa* is one of many famous paintings found at the Louvre.

## Local Art Fairs

Many cities host art fairs. Art fairs allow local artists to showcase and sell their work. These fairs help smaller artists find an audience. People can support local artists by buying their work.

Many museums around the world have interactive art exhibits where people can experience paintings in new ways. One of the most popular interactive exhibits features works from famous painter Vincent van Gogh.

The National Gallery in London, the United Kingdom, is another popular place to see paintings. So is the National Art Center in Tokyo, Japan.

Most paintings do not end up in museums. People everywhere paint pictures to express themselves. Whether someone is a professional or a new artist, trying new mediums and styles can be fun!

## Explore Online

Visit the website below. Does it give any new information about Frida Kahlo that wasn't in Chapter Three?

### Frida Kahlo

abdocorelibrary.com/art-of-painting

# Art Supplies

Paint

Paintbrushes

Canvas
Palette

# Glossary

**abstract**
general shapes and colors that achieve an effect rather than realistically representing a subject

**bleed**
to flow out of or away from something

**canvas**
a strong type of fabric that artists can paint on

**dimension**
the depth, height, or width of an object

**mental illness**
a range of medical conditions that affect the way a person thinks or feels

**opaque**
not see-through

**palette**
a board or tablet that holds paint

**warp**
to twist or curve something out of its original shape

# Online Resources

To learn more about painting, visit our free resource websites below.

Visit **abdocorelibrary.com** or scan this QR code for free Common Core resources for teachers and students, including vetted activities, multimedia, and booklinks, for deeper subject comprehension.

Visit **abdobooklinks.com** or scan this QR code for free additional online weblinks for further learning. These links are routinely monitored and updated to provide the most current information available.

# Learn More

Conley, Kate. *Frida Kahlo*. Abdo, 2022.

Meltzer, Brad. *I Am Leonardo da Vinci*. Dial Books for Young Readers, 2020.

Murray, Julie. *Impressionism*. Abdo, 2024.

# Index



# About the Author

Marley Richmond is a children's book editor and author. She lives in Minnesota with her cat, Bean. Marley's mom taught her to paint, and they still enjoy making art together.